JOAN
CHITTISTER

❀ FOREWORD *by* PAULA D'ARCY ❀

ASPECTS
OF THE

heart

❁

The MANY PATHS *to a* GOOD LIFE

2414
CHI

For more information about
Joan Chittister, OSB, please visit her
website: www.joanchittister.org

TWENTY-THIRD PUBLICATIONS
A Division of Bayard
One Montauk Avenue, Suite 200
New London, CT 06320
(860) 437-3012 or (800) 321-0411
www.23rdpublications.com

ISBN 978-1-58595-871-9
Library of Congress Control Number: 2012942438

Printed in the U.S.A.

CONTENTS

FOREWORD

It was years ago, my life bursting with grief at the sudden loss of my husband and daughter in an automobile accident, that I first met the power of the human heart. Finding the heart's "yes," its willingness not only to go on but to fully meet the great force of love moving through life, was a great challenge. Only decades later would someone use words that underscored that moment: *There are two things of great importance in life: Your intention and the opening of the heart.*

Unfortunately, there are no notes on this in school. To learn about the human heart, we all rely on life experiences and the guides we meet along the way. Eventually some of us begin to investigate for ourselves, allowing the journey to bring many things into question. Whether or not we decide to go deeper, none of us are exempt from the heart's invitation. At times the heart shouts its wisdom, but very often it assists us so quietly that we're at risk of not hearing its voice at all. One thing seems clear: To help the movement of love find its way in this world, we must develop a different and deeper relationship with the heart. We must risk our own vulnerability and respond to the heart's beckoning. We must learn that whatever takes us to the limits of our strength is there for our own sake.

In these beautiful and spare reflections, Joan invites us to sit at the world's table and decide what our hearts will offer. She wisely reminds the reader that "there is no such thing as an isolated act." We are each responsible for "doing everything we can to make the world whole." Still, it's not necessary to do something heroic. In making a pilgrimage to the heart, we don't initially struggle with world issues and injustices; we wrestle first with the love struggling to break through our own unique circumstances. We notice how easily and reflexively the heart begins to close when we feel threatened in any way. We notice that bringing love when we confront hatred, as St. Francis prays, is not for the faint of heart. But the result of our effort to meet life fully is that we ourselves become the space through which love can move in the world. We only have to do one thing: Let the heart call us back to love.

These pages will help you recognize many characteristics of the heart: *A kind heart. A humble heart. A non-judgmental heart. A celebrating heart. A trusting heart...* They will assure you that the storms of life are the very place to look for God. They will offer the wisdom that "real peace requires resistance to evil. But not in evil ways." They will show that you must "risk becoming new." They will help you acknowledge and value the treasury that is yours.

Under Joan's expert and prophetic pen these powerful reflections are like an owner's manual for understanding the power of the heart and the force of love. Her accumulated wisdom becomes the sub-text that reminds us that even though dedicated practice and saying "yes" to love won't make our problems go away, it *will* help us recognize Light as it moves through the darkness, able to penetrate our struggles when they come. In the act of opening the heart, the deep, altering stillness of God begins to move. Live to the limits of your heart, Joan tells us. Since she continues to do this with her own life, these offerings have great power. Spoken from the authenticity of her considerable contribution to the world, her admonition "Today is the whole of life. Don't miss it" becomes the guiding voice of these potent teachings. Slow down, she reminds us. Look around. Live life deeply. It is open to us all.   PAULA D'ARCY

The heart

**A good person produces good from
the treasure of the heart.** LUKE 6:45

EVERYTHING WE DO IN LIFE, the Scripture reminds us, goes into the treasury of the heart. The ideas with which we fill our hearts determine the way we live our lives. Those are the things we draw on in those moments when we need to reach down deep inside ourselves for character, courage, endurance, and hope. That's why what we read, what we see, and what we do from day to day counts so much in life.

The heart is not an arrow. It is an amalgam of magnets, all pulling in different directions. It is commitment to family, commitment to self, commitment to success, commitment to life, commitment to God, commitment to security, commitment to approval—all jangled and knotted and demanding.

Goodness is the ability to choose one over the other when it counts.

And when does it really count? It counts when someone else's life will suffer if we do not muster the courage to make the right choice in this situation at this time in this place.

The onetime Buddhist patriarch of Cambodia, Maha Ghosananda, saw his entire family killed by the Khmer Rouge. And he is the one who initiated the Walks for Peace through the Khmer Rouge countryside in the hope of bringing the country to reconciliation. Now that's goodness.

Courage can be a hidden virtue. Faith can be personal. Goodness is the kind of character trait, however, that cannot be practiced alone. Goodness requires a public posture. To be good you have to be good to someone else. And most essential of all, perhaps, to the nature of goodness is the fact that not to choose—not to get involved, not to decide, not to bother—is the most serious choice of all.

An attentive heart

**Let us so live that when we come to die
even the undertaker will be sorry.**

MARK TWAIN

IT IS ONE THING TO BE GIVEN LIFE BY GOD.
It is another thing to live it in a way that is a tribute
to the possibilities in life.

While we're working so hard and running so fast
and buying so much and planning "for the future,"
today passes us by. Life passes us by. It becomes a
list of things we'd like to do—but don't: see the plays,
visit the relatives, invite neighbors to a barbecue, sit
by the bank and fish, listen to the small, still voice of
God in our hearts. But if that's the case, what are all
those other things really about?

For life to be life, I must do at least one thing a
day for my soul, one thing a day for my heart, one

thing a day for my mind. Count them every day for a month and you'll know what's missing in you when you hear yourself say, "There's something not quite right in me but I don't know what it is."

The key to today is to live it well, live it happily, live it with surprise. Something good is coming. All we have to do is to recognize it when it does. The good life is the life in which every single strain of it has been lived with a good heart, an open mind, and the faith that tells us that God is behind every new and different door.

Today is the whole of life. Don't miss it.

A broken heart

A rabbi always told his people that if they studied the Torah, it would put Scripture on their hearts. One of them asked, "Why 'on' our hearts and not 'in' them?"

The rabbi answered, "Only God can put Scripture inside. But reading sacred text can put it on your hearts, and then when the heart breaks open, the holy words will fall inside."

SO MANY THINGS BREAK A HEART open in life. Sudden bursts of beauty lift the scales from our eyes. We begin to see differently. A rose enduring through early winter snow can do it every time.

A graveyard agony is sure to stop our stride a bit, make us think again about what life is about, shake us to our moorings.

Passion turns life a brighter gold than we ever

imagined it could be. It leaves us full of wonder, full of faith, full of the consciousness of a smiling universe.

Long, slow, unyielding burdens—a child whose problem no one can name, a purse forever thin, distance where we would hope for help—can be a challenge. Eventually the heart dries out from the lack of nurture, and the fissures begin to form. Then what happens to us? The rabbi in the story says it all depends on what we have been putting on our hearts all these years. If it is the Scripture, we will know that God is with us now as God has always been active in the world since the beginning of time. If we have stayed close to the story of God's presence in life, we can bear any burden, survive any loss, absorb however much beauty without dying from the breathless glory of it, and give ourselves to the other side of love—the side that gives as well as takes.

A celebrating heart

**One of the very nicest things about life
is the way we must regularly stop whatever it is we
are doing and devote our attention to eating.**

LUCIANO PAVAROTTI

IF YOU WANT TO KNOW whether or not you're living a balanced life, ask yourself whether your feasting and your fasting—your sense of praise and trust—come in common measure.

Learning to celebrate life is one of the best lessons a person can learn. Celebrations are an excuse to enjoy the world and to enable others to enjoy it too. When we dot our lives with unscheduled as well as scheduled feast days, we remember that we are able to make joy as well as to expect it.

In this country we are conditioned to think that taking time to eat together, to make a meal an event rather than an act, takes time from the important things in our life. That may be exactly why we are so confused now about what the important things of life really are. To love good food is a measure of our love of life. Food preparation teaches us to do everything we can do to make life palatable, spicy, comforting, full of love.

The oyster stew and the watermelon, the fresh bread for sandwiches and the bottle of wine to go with them, the smell of a Christmas ham and a turkey on Thanksgiving, the weekly meal with the crowd, and the holidays and birthdays and picnics and family specialties all serve to remind us still of the glory of God, the bounty of God, the blessedness of life, the proof that life, in the end, is always good.

To be feasted is to be loved outrageously. Feasting is a divine imperative. It says, "Thou shalt not ignore the joys of life."

A compassionate heart

**The capacity to care is what gives life
its deepest significance.** PABLO CASALS

IT IS EASY TO BE RELIGIOUS; it is difficult to
be spiritual. A religious life requires that we be just
to the other. The spiritual life demands that we be
compassionate to the other.

To be deeply spiritual, wholly compassionate, we
must remember that the one in need is simply another version of ourselves that we may have yet to
meet in life but someday surely will.

The world will not heal itself. Only a compassionate heart can do that.

Compassion oils the astronomy of the human
condition. It brings us into touch with one another,
finds the light in each, and magnifies it to the point
that the world brightens with a new kind of under-

standing, a better kind of human community.

Knowledge does very little for life. It is compassion that makes it livable, compassion that gives it the kind of vision that gives us all a reason to be alive.

No one of us is here for ourselves alone. That is the single most important lesson of life. Compassion, to be real, must be universal, not selective. I cannot claim to be compassionate if I leave anyone outside the boundaries of my care. Only if my heart is large enough and my vision wide enough can I ever hope to be bigger than my own small agenda. Then I have something worth living for, giving to, suffering with, forever. Then I am a gift to the rest of humankind.

A connected heart

**Each small task of everyday life is
part of the total harmony of the universe.**

ST. THÉRÈSE OF LISIEUX

HINDUISM TEACHES THAT EVERYTHING in creation comes from the breaking of the Divine Egg. We are all, therefore, fragments of the Divine and related to everything else in life.

There is no such thing as an isolated act. It isn't true that nothing I do matters, that I am powerless, that I have nothing to do with the big things in life. Without the little things, the big things in life fail—like marriage and world peace and the ecosystem.

What we ourselves do not do well cannot possibly be done by someone else. That's why everything we do—washing dishes, babysitting, donating food, visiting the elderly, helping a coworker, sharing a gift, tending the yard—is so important.

There is no such thing as being "neutral." We are either for something and so promote it, or we are against something and resist it. Even doing nothing is doing something. By our silence we either encourage or obstruct exactly what we claim to be neutral about.

Harmony is not a matter of refusing to participate and so refusing to do our part in the world. It is a matter of doing everything we can to make the world whole. We are not worlds unto ourselves, indivisible parts in orbit around one another. And yet, every person we pass in a hallway is affected by us one way or another. We either pollute or we perfume an atmosphere. There is no other choice.

Once we see that everything is connected, we see the purpose of life. Our own and everybody else's.

A converting heart

To insist on a spiritual practice that served you in the past is to carry the raft on your back after you have crossed the river. BUDDHA

CHANGE IS VERY DIFFICULT. It requires us to accept with open arms and a trusting heart that the God who sustained us yesterday will still be here tomorrow.

Not even the spiritual life is changeless. On the contrary, nothing really requires more humility from us than the willingness to open ourselves to the unknown so that God can complete in us what has been begun.

Letting go of what we have come to depend on is never easy. But it is always growthful. It keeps us young and vibrant and engaged. It makes us important rather than just stuffy. Holy instead of simply self-righteous.

When we simply close our minds to new possibilities—without even bothering to reflect on the new questions out of which new forms are emerging—we entomb ourselves in a very small world called fear and control and spiritual sclerosis.

Conversion is what enables us to become the best of ourselves. It frees us from what has us enslaved. Human growth is neither absolute nor certain. It is a voyage into the jungle of the self with the intention of finding a way out of it, stronger, fuller, and more peaceful than ever before. It is the adventure of a lifetime. As the desert master Abba Poeman said about Abba Pior, "Every single day he makes a fresh beginning."

A cosmic heart

I have learned so much from God that I can no longer call myself a Christian, a Hindu, a Muslim, a Buddhist, a Jew. The truth has shared so much of itself with me that I no longer think of myself as a man, a woman, an angel, or even pure soul. Existence has become so saturated with laughter it has freed me of every concept and image a mind could ever war with.

HAFIZ, TRAN. DANIEL LADINSKY

GOD SPEAKS IN MANY TONGUES, glows in many colors, calls to us in many voices, and is beyond any puny, little, parochial image we make of God. It is this great cosmic God we seek.

To recognize God in others is to extend the boundaries of the self. Then God and we are not a world to ourselves. We are simply a missing piece in the glories of the universe.

When we begin to understand that God is everywhere, in everyone, alive in the world always, then life becomes a joy, not a burden, and other people a sign of possibility, not danger. Then we learn to laugh again.

A life filled with the awareness of God, a sense of the security of God, and an appreciation of the creativity of God is a life full of the laughter that comes from knowing that everything is holy and, eventually, everything will also come out right.

How do I know if I'm finally becoming closer to God? Easy. It's when I see God in everyone I meet and touch God in everything that is.

How do we know if the religion we say we hold so dear and believe so deeply and practice so well is really as developed in us as we think it is? Nick Annis wrote, "Here's a tip: If you're killing someone in the name of God—you're missing the message."

A creative heart

Work is love made visible, and if you cannot work with love but only with distaste, it is better that you should leave your work and sit at the gate of the temple and take alms of those who work with joy. KAHLIL GIBRAN

EACH OF US IS HERE to participate in the creativity of God by adding something of ourselves to creation.

Good work, creative work, is any work that makes the world around us a better, more humane place to be. It isn't just creating something new that makes us "creative." It is taking care of what is good in it that makes us artists of our own lives. What we do to beautify the world is a service of the soul that touches the souls around us as well as fulfills our own.

It is impossible to do anything that affects only ourselves. Every good we do makes the world better.

Every harm we do, even to ourselves, makes it worse for someone else. Work, for its own sake, is not necessarily good. Drug dealers work; weapons sellers work; computer hackers work. No, to be good work, it must be work that means no harm to others.

To work at what we love to do is a kind of richness no salary at another kind of work can possibly provide. It's one thing to make a living; it's another thing to make a life.

Even in prison, doing a work we love can grow the soul and save a person. The Bird Man of Alcatraz subverted the entire system of his incarceration by taming the birds on his windowsills rather than allowing himself to waste his entire life on bitterness and depression. When we do something beautiful, we become beautiful ourselves.

To do our work—whatever it is, however small, however hidden—the best we can raises the quality of life for everyone around us. Productive work enhances the world; creative work enriches the world; holy work makes the world a better place for all of us.

A desiring heart

**In this world there are two tragedies.
One is not getting what one wants,
and the other is getting it.**

OSCAR WILDE

PART OF BEING HUMAN is the fine art of learning how not to be in control. That is the link that binds us to God—leaving omniscience where it belongs. There is something charming in the process of trying to coax God. If only we realized that it is not coaxing God that counts. It is learning to face reality ourselves that makes the difference between spiritual childhood and spiritual adulthood.

Just remember this: No matter what you think you want, what you get will be exactly what you need at the time.

Don't be afraid to want something. Wanting is a

precious part of being human. It carries us from one moment to the next, from one period of life to another. Human expectations, achieved or not, are the signal inside of us that we know God is not remote, not disinterested in human life, but actually nearby and the giver of everything we need.

The broken hearts we bear are almost always of our own breaking. We want what we have no right to expect. It is the way of coming to fullness of life. "I can hear the philosophers protesting that it can only be misery to live in folly, illusion, deception and ignorance," Erasmus wrote, "but it isn't—it's human." When what we want we do not get, we have the opportunity to develop something else. Dampened expectations are the beginning of a healthy journey to new ideas, new interests, new events.

A discerning heart

If you come to a fork in the road, take it.

YOGI BERRA

LIFE'S GREAT DECISIONS ARE ALL HIDDEN behind a veil that makes it impossible for us to see the results of them.

All choice is crisis in the Chinese sense of the word. It is both danger and opportunity. It is when we see only one of these polarities that we are more than likely to make a bad decision in the choice.

Against danger we must always be prepared. In the face of opportunity, we must never say "impossible."

It isn't, in most cases, that we don't know which road we want to take. It's simply that we waste our lives wanting a guarantee of it.

Indeed, the big decisions in life are hardly ever

clear. But one thing is: Life is a series of dilemmas, of options, of conundrums, of possibilities taken and not taken. Good decision, bad decision, who knows? What makes the difference between them? Only this: It is the values that we bring to the decision-making process and the attitude we take into the living out of them that turn the crossroads into new life.

They made fun of Yogi Berra for his seemingly senseless insight, but he wasn't all wrong. Crossroads are those moments in life when we get the opportunity—when we have no other choice but to begin again. Indeed, "if you come to a fork in the road," take it with an open heart. Trust that the Spirit that brought you this far will not abandon you on the way.

A doubting heart

Faith is the bird that sings when the dawn is still dark. RABINDRANATH TAGORE

JUST BECAUSE WE SAY WE BELIEVE does not protect us from the saving grace of doubt. In fact, if anything, it tests us. Doubt is a necessary exercise in the confession of faith. It is sure proof that the soul seeks more than what's there.

Doubt is not always a burden. It can save us from arrogance, from superiority, and from pride. It can make eagles out of sheep. It enables us to be skeptical of scams and wary of rug sellers. It makes us thinking people.

Doubt is the call to trust our instincts, our feelings, and our faith more than we trust a collection of constantly changing "facts." There is no need for faith when everything is clear and comfortable and constant. Faith is what we need when we discover that we are not in charge of our world. And that can take years to realize.

Faith is not certainty. It is simply the clear awareness that there must be more to what is happening than I can see or change and, therefore, for me, is the will of God now.

"The dark night of the soul," that period of growth when none of our past beliefs seem certain anymore, may bring us closer to God than we have ever been in our lives. Then our souls become focused, strained, on finding the light again.

Doubt and faith are essential to one another. Doubt is what makes faith mature. The very pursuit of the questions faith demands is what moves us beyond magic to the mystery of God.

An enduring heart

**Lead, kindly Light,
amid the encircling gloom,
lead Thou me on.**

JOHN HENRY NEWMAN

CATHERINE OF SIENA TAUGHT, "Nothing was done without much enduring." The trouble is that we are all inclined to quit a thing too quickly. We quit when people tell us we'll never make it. We quit when we get tired. We quit when we don't improve. These criteria slow a lot of human progress. Worse than that, factors such as these limit our own development.

Staying with a difficult situation to resolve it, rather than trying to escape it, gives God the chance to complete what such an experience was meant to effect in us. Survival is a by-product of trust. When we flail our way through life, the effort of it gets to be too much for us. It's learning to rest in the arms of the Creator that takes us through what could otherwise have destroyed us.

The point is that everything we survive in life provides us with one more layer of humanity with which to live it.

The nature of things we endure are the things that define our own character. Endurance is not a virtue when it tolerates evil. "If we had been holier people," Templeton wrote, "we would have been angrier oftener." Which means: Never endure what is not in itself essentially good, or designed to make everybody's world a better place, or, in the end, really good for your own development. To violate any of those things is to violate the will of God for creation.

An evolving heart

The only man I know who behaves sensibly is my tailor; he takes my measurements anew each time he sees me. The rest go on with their old measurements and expect me to fit them.

GEORGE BERNARD SHAW

ASSUMING THAT TOMORROW will be the same as today is poor preparation for living. It equips us only for disappointment or shock. To live well, to be mentally healthy, we must learn to realize that life is a work in progress.

Life happens in small stages. The quantum leaps in life—great new promotions, stunning losses—even when they happen, take a lot of growing into if we are to become what they exact in us.

Because change is of the essence of life, we know that anything is possible. The only thing we don't know is what it will do to us. "Change is the constant," Christina Baldwin wrote, "the signal for rebirth, the egg of the phoenix." All we really need to learn to do is to accept the present with open arms and let it do what it must to us.

Nothing is stable in life. Nothing can be taken for granted. Nothing is static. Everything goes on changing. Sometimes in great, bold, striking ways. Sometimes in tiny little incremental changes that sneak up on us unaware—like weight and height and age. Don't be afraid of becoming different than you are—just be sure you enjoy the gifts of each and every stage as well as bemoan its burdens.

Life just goes on demanding new life from us all the time.

The spiritual task is to keep measuring the shades of difference that are all around us in life and keep adjusting to them.

A free heart

**I know but one freedom and
that is the freedom of the mind.**

ANTOINE DE SAINT-EXUPÉRY

WHEN WE GIVE AWAY OUR RIGHT to think for
ourselves, we lose the possibility of ever coming to
fullness of life.

It's so easy to pose as a thinker when what we
really are is a consumer of someone else's thoughts—
my husband's maybe; my pastor's perhaps; my
mother's, for instance. When we copy the opinions
of another, repeat the ideas of others, critique nothing, cut no new mental paths for ourselves, swallow
the world like whole cloth, we are not only enslaved;
we are clones of those around us, pretending to be
human.

To take the freedom it requires to be myself, to

say my ideas aloud, to be strong enough to confront someone else's ideas, means that we claim the right to contribute to the scope and richness of the human enterprise.

We are so afraid to be different from those whose company we seek. But what is the use of my being with them if the real me is not really with them at all. Then we are both denied. I am denied the right to be me. They are denied the right to be influenced by me as I am by them.

Everyone of us is meant to stand for something sometimes in life—to risk ridicule, to bear opposition, to believe differently in the face of those who believe otherwise. And that is often a very lonesome road, peopled only by those free of the seductions of human approval.

But that is the kind of freedom—freedom from the self, freedom for the gospel—that changes things.

A gifted heart

**When someone asks what there is to do,
light the candle in their hand.**

RUMI

TO KNOW OUR GIFTS is to know our role in life.
We are what we are. But the gift of self unfolds as
we go, often slowly, always with surprise. It can take
years before it becomes clear—the real gift that is
hidden within us. Finding the gifts that God has
given you takes courage; it takes risk; it takes explo-
ration; it takes failure as we stumble from one arena
to the other. But in the end what I get back is the
wholeness of myself.

We all come with a gift in our hand designed
to make life a better place. The only question is
whether we spend it on others or only on ourselves.

It is learning that the gifts we have been given

are given for the rest of the human community that makes us more human ourselves. Everyone does some things better than other things. What I have to give is always that one thing that is most needed in every situation because no one else can give it. The obligation is to pour it out like oil on the head of the universe.

Don't be afraid to follow the dreams of your heart. They are the sign of what should be, of what you must do to be whole, of what you down deep really believe the world must taste to be true to itself.

Without you and me and our little gift, the world will never be filled up. Asked to write a letter to the *London Times* on "What's wrong with the world?" GK Chesterton wrote, "Dear Sirs, I am. Yours truly, GK Chesterton." Clearly, what we are asked to give is only what we are—and that is more than nothing.

A grieving heart

Spill tears if you have grief
As tears of grief provide relief.

SHA'WANA, SUFI MYSTIC

GRIEF IS THAT SLICE OF LIFE that takes us beyond the boundaries of our mind and makes us see life anew again. It is possible that when life is just the way we like it, life is far, far too small to do what life is really meant to do.

Grief grows us up. When we come to understand that whatever we have we can lose, we begin, first, to hold everything lightly, and, second, we learn to squeeze happiness dry.

The little losses of life prepare us to survive the great ones. We find out little by little as we go through one small change after another that it is possible after loss—no matter how initially bottomless the pit—to laugh again, to love again, to begin again. Practice savoring your little losses. They may be what save you in the end.

To tell a person in grief not to grieve may be the unkindest cut of all. It denies them the right to re-evaluate their lives, to treasure their past, and to be accompanied through their new fears. Because we are not prepared to deal with the reality of loss, we want no one else to face it either.

Grief is a process of many stages and no guaranteed cutoff points. When something happens that in our minds should not have happened—a child dies, a group betrays us, a loved one leaves—there is no charting the time it will take to recover. There is only the sure knowledge that we can recover if for no other reason than that so many have.

Once we realize that everything we touch is in the act of disappearing, we shall touch it more intensely. The very thought of grief prepares us to live well.

A heart for beauty

It is finished in beauty.
It is finished in beauty.

NAVAJO CHANT

BEAUTY TAKES MANY FORMS. I have seen them, disarmingly simple and boldly compelling, both where I expected them and where I did not. I saw a Mexican Indian woman, nine members of her family assassinated in the mountains of Chiapas, stand at their grave site, infant in arms, hard-jawed but soft of eye and still open to life. That was beautiful.

I watched, too, as lines and lines of working-class Italians stood waiting for hours for the coarse lights to go on that would illuminate, for too precious a moment, Michelangelo's "Moses" in the small, dark chapel of St. Peter in Chains in Rome. The awe in their eyes was as beautiful as the sinews in the marbled arms, the big-boned kneecaps of the Moses above them. Both were full of feeling; both held promise of the kind of energy that can come only from the depths of the human heart.

Once I stood, hands clasped behind me, and stared at eye level into Rembrandt's "The Flight into Egypt," black on black on black, one small light glowing in the darkness of exile. That was beauty beyond beauty, the vision of someone who had seen more in the wilderness of flight than I had ever known was there.

Beauty is a deeply spiritual experience. It shouts to us always, "More. There is yet more." We cannot hope for fullness of life without nurturing fullness of soul. We must seek beauty, study beauty, surround ourselves with beauty. To revivify the soul, the world, we must become beauty.

A heart for nature

**The trees and the stones will teach you
what you never learn from the masters.**

BERNARD OF CLAIRVAUX

To CULTIVATE AN APPRECIATION OF NATURE
is to deepen our own spiritual life, to come closer to
creation, to see our own moral responsibility to it
in the way we treat every blade of grass. To live in
harmony with nature is to be more alive ourselves.

Our synchronicity with nature is demonstrated
by the emotional effect it has on us. When it's dark,
so can we become morose. When mist hangs in the
mountains around us, when the fog sets in, so do
we become reflective. When the sun is burning the
stones, every nerve comes alive in us. Each change
is nature calling us to go deeper into the rhythms
of life. It is seeing ourselves as part of nature rather

than outside of it that attunes the soul to the teachings of nature.

We do not "control" nature. Nature controls us. The only problem is that it takes a modern, industrial world generations to understand that. When we destroy nature without the implications of what we are doing to the future, nature always has the last word. Look at what we are doing to the earth, and you will know what changes we need to make in our own lives if we are to be truly seekers of God.

Walking through nature, we walk hand in hand with God who enlivened it. The only question is: Shall we bring it life or death? In one of her visions, Hildegard of Bingen, 12th-century mystic, says of nature: "I am that living and fiery essence of the divine substance....I shine in the water; I burn in the sun and the moon and the stars." Oh, to live long enough and well enough to come to see those things ourselves.

A heart that remembers

**Memory...is the diary
that we all carry about with us.**

OSCAR WILDE

WE ALL CARRY THINGS FROM THE PAST that determine how we live life, what we think about things, how we feel about people, how we look at the world. "I am part of all that I have met," the poet says. Maybe we would all understand everyone else better if we only asked now what it is from the past that brought us to this point.

Some of those things may be blocking our capacity to experience all of life now. On the other hand, they may be exactly what make us open to it.

The saddest thing in life may be the tendency to think that my present judgments come out of my present experience, have real currency now, are the result of well thought-out positions, are really rational or appropriate to today. To do that is to freeze ourselves in time.

Deciding which ideas to carry forward in life determines what kind of person we will be in the end: a reactionary (the kind of person who trusts the God of yesterday but not the God of tomorrow), or a revolutionary (the kind of person who believes that our creating God goes on creating what we need from age to age).

The important thing is to remember that my memories are only signs of the possible; they are not absolutes. They give me a sense of possibility, not a guarantee of anything. Personal growth is the ability to test them out.

A hopeful heart

Those who lose dreaming are lost.

ABORIGINAL PROVERB

THE KINDS OF DREAMS WE HAVE determine the quality of our lives. The problem is not that we don't dream. The problem is that we seldom dream high enough.

What we dream about we will surely get—or at least some pale facsimile of it. What is important is not getting the dream but being able to appraise it once it is within reach. To dream without being willing to do something ourselves to make the dream come true dooms us to a life that never comes to fruit.

When we stop pursuing a dream before the dream is clearly impossible, we fail to pursue our own best development. Then we have to ask what it is that is really blocking us: fear, insecurity, lack of initiative, or lack of faith?

What we are inclined to call in our realistic old age "the dreams of youth" may be the saddest commentary a person can make on the state of the human soul. Dreams don't die in youth; they are simply abandoned there for the sake of a deceit we call "realism." Dreams are not only for the young. Dreams make every stage of life the great adventure it is meant to be.

The nice thing about a dream is that we never get exactly what we set out to achieve—which means that there are always things left over to pursue when the journey of life goes dark. Not to have a dream for tomorrow, for next year, for life is to abandon myself not simply to chance but to life without a rudder. Show me a dreamer and I'll show you one of God's heartbeats for the human race.

A hospitable heart

**If it were not for guests,
all houses would be graves.**

KAHLIL GIBRAN

TO BE OPEN TO THE WORLD is a dangerous way
to live. It threatens us with learning things we've
always been taught to reject. What we don't know,
we are inclined to fear. Embalmed in sameness, we
lose the opportunity to grow into what life means
to become.

When we go out of ourselves to make a connection with the other; we not only attend to the
needs of the other, we become more than we were
when we began. Hospitality of the heart works
both ways.

Hospitality of the heart is what makes the world
a tender and lovely place to be. It is what makes in-

terdependence real. As much as we all need one another in material ways, we also need one another in more ways than physical ones. From one end of the globe to the other, we look to one another for understanding, for insight and support.

Hospitality is a willingness to be imposed upon for the sake of the other's well-being. It is the sacrament of the self. It is far and above beyond the boundaries of mere socializing. It is the heartfelt awareness of another's needs and the determination to serve them.

Solitude is a human need; distance is a human problem; hospitality is the human gift that bridges the two. When people come into our lives, they come bearing insights, wisdom, traditions, cultures, and ideas that stretch us to the limit. They come bringing us the opportunity to become fully developed human beings.

A human heart

**In the book of life,
the answers aren't in the back.**

CHARLIE BROWN, CHARLES SCHULTZ

LIFE IS WHAT WE LEARN AS WE LIVE IT. And it is what we learn as we live it that tests and shapes the mettle of our souls.

There is no way to comprehend how to go through grief other than by going through it. There is no way to practice foregoing the hot rage that comes with feeling ignored or dismissed for any reason. There is no way to plan for the sense of abandonment you feel in a society that thinks differently from you: because your child is gay, maybe, or because you're a woman and so automatically considered deficient for the work, perhaps, or because you're not white in a white world, or because the person you thought was an eternal friend left you.

These things we need to figure out for ourselves, one situation at a time.

But then, once we have been through those dark and raw moments in life, we discover a newer, better kind of sweetness. We not only find out who other people are; we find out what we are, too. We find out not only how weak we feel but how strong we can really be in the face of endless pain or mockery or bigotry or the shallowness of self-righteous morality.

Then, we discover that life is not a terminal disease. On the contrary, it is always, and at best, a time of endless development, of choosing to be either more or less than we thought we could be. It's not a matter of going through life; it is a matter of growing steadily deeper, always broader, forever wiser.

A humble heart

Do your work, then step back.
The only path to serenity.

LAO TSU

AT THE END OF THE DAY, we discover that humility—the strength to separate our sense of the meaning of life from what we do—is the only real answer to lifelong happiness.

Humility is the cultivation of the strength it takes to admit I'm wrong, I don't know, I made a mistake. It makes it possible for a person to begin again. Pride is weakness. It pretends to have what I do not—and exposes me to the public who know better than that.

Pride focuses on externals. Humility springs from an internal well.

Humility refuses to wear a mask. The humble person knows who they are and tells someone else

50

in order to guard themselves against the tempta-tion to pretention. Pride is the process of fooling ourselves, of posturing for the sake of others, of pretending to be who and what we are not. It is the worst kind of slavery.

There is a good pride that takes more pleasure in the aspiration—in the desire—to do good and do it well than in the achievement itself. Good pride is not so much a need to heap up rewards as it is rec-ognition of the diligence that has brought me to this place. The truly humble never really covet recogni-tion. They simply accept it, if and when it comes, and wear it lightly.

Humility is the height of inner freedom. It is in thrall to no one and nothing, not even its own self-image. Only the humble are truly happy. There is nothing they have that anyone can take from them, and all that they have, whatever it is, they enjoy for its own sake.

An imperfect heart

**This is the very perfection of a person,
to find out our own imperfections.**

ST. AUGUSTINE

HUMANITY IS A MIXTURE OF BLUNDERS. That's what makes it so charming, so interesting to be around. Because none of us is complete, we all need one another. It's only when we convince ourselves that we are the fullness of all that is, that we become spiritually poor.

The nice thing about being human is that you get to fail a lot. Value that; it's priceless. It gives us such respect for everybody else. The reason clowns and slapstick comedians are so popular is that, if truth were known, we all see in them the parts of ourselves we try too hard to hide. When we take ourselves too seriously, we forget that the only thing we know for sure that's eternal is God.

Making mistakes is part of the growth process. We must learn to be much gentler about this with other people. We must also learn to be gentler with ourselves. Otherwise, what we expect of ourselves, we will expect of everybody else. And that can be tragic. For all of us.

Never be afraid to admit that you "don't know" or "can't find" or "couldn't do" something. Our imperfections and inabilities are the only thing we have that gives us the right to the support of the rest of the human race.

The gift of knowing what we lack is the gift we have to give to the abilities of others. As the Irish proverb says, "It is in the shelter of each other that the people live."

An intimate heart

I find it shelter to speak to you.

EMILY DICKINSON

A FRIEND IS MORE THAN AN ACQUAINTANCE. A friend is a soul-partner at every age, the one who looks at us and says, "I know exactly who you are and I love you for it. I know what all the others do not know and I love you, both because of it and despite it." There is nothing closer or more meaningful in life than intimacy.

The way to cultivate a friendship is to be prepared both to talk and to listen for the rest of your life. "Good talk is pure gold and it's what lovers need from each other," wrote Garrison Keillor

People who do not allow us to say what we truly believe, who do not care what we really feel about anything, are not our friends. They are, at best, acquaintances who should have gone home a long time ago.

There are moments of loneliness in every life. Moments when what needs to be said has no one to say it—or at least no one who can understand its real meaning or import. Then it is better to be silent and wait for someone to come into our lives who can hear what we're trying to say without having to say it. The one who simply understands us so well that it's not necessary to say much at all.

It is one thing to have a friend; it is another thing to be one. It means that I am promising to put my own schedule and work and busyness and interests aside in order to immerse myself in yours. It is a gift of rarest beauty, of deepest meaning, of truest love.

An invested heart

**Only those who dare to fail greatly
can ever achieve greatly.**

ROBERT KENNEDY

WHAT WE ARE AT THE CORE OF US determines what we spend our life doing.

All the effort in the world does not guarantee that we will accomplish what we set out to achieve. It does guarantee a stimulating life. All the effort I spend to make my world better may not change a thing in my lifetime, but it can make it possible for someone else to do it later.

We must always have something to grasp for that is worth the effort. Otherwise, there is no reason to be alive. But we must never have so much to grasp for that it's impossible to achieve. Otherwise, there is no reason to try.

It's not really how much of my life a thing will cost me to get it that counts in the end. It is whether or not it's really worth that much to begin with. What we pay for a thing with our life must be worthy of a life.

Truth, goodness, and beauty, the philosophers told us, are the most valuable things in life. For those things, we must be willing to pay any price at all. And John of the Cross reminds us, "In the evening of life, we will be judged on love alone." Not on earthly possession or human success.

It is spending our lives on what is worthwhile that is the measure of our greatness.

A joyful heart

**We choose our joys and sorrows
long before we experience them.**

KAHLIL GIBRAN

TOO OFTEN WE WAIT FOR JOY to come to us when the real truth is that joy is something we must take responsibility for creating, not just for ourselves but for others as well. The beauty of joy is that, like a stained glass window through which light breaks into a myriad of colors, it enables us to see how good life is, even when it seems that it isn't. Joy is not an event; it is the attitude a healthy person takes into every situation in life—work, family, social life, and even moments of personal stress. It speaks of hope and openness, of enticing possibility and the deep conviction that what is given to us in life is given to us for our own good.

The person who is spiritually mature trusts in the presence of a loving God to bring this moment, whatever it is, to ripen in the soul. It is through the lens of joy that we must learn to look at all of life. All of it is good but some of it we don't recognize when it happens.

To be really holy people, we must stop thinking of joy as an accident of nature and begin to make it a priority. "Always remember," Rebbe Nachman of Breslov taught, "joy is not incidental to your spiritual quest. It is vital."

And the ancients remind us, "There's no such thing as a sad saint." Never confuse holiness with rigidity, morbidity, or moodiness. Those come from preoccupation with self, not with any awareness of the presence of God.

A kind heart

**To give pleasure to a single heart
by a single kind act is better than a
thousand head-bowings in prayer.**

SAADI

WHAT IS KINDNESS? It is a tendency of care, for which all the skill in the world cannot suffice.

Kindness is not recompense for favors received; it is unearned warmth given for absolutely no reason at all. The kindnesses we remember are the ones that saved us from the straits we were otherwise incapable of leaping over by ourselves.

To be kind is to be equally approachable in all situations. Hard times are hard enough without our adding to them by making it even more difficult for people to survive the difficulties.

Kindness in the midst of pain is salvific. It heals

60

the sick and strengthens the weak and gives hope to the depressed. It makes another week, another day, another hour possible.

To be kind does not mean that we must be weak. It means that we have the strength it takes to be ourselves without having to hurt others in the process.

No one fears a person who is kind. Everyone feels safe with the person who is kind. Kindness make friends of us all. To be consistently gentle and kind in the way we deal with people is a greater gift than any other gift we have to give. We often talk about "loving one another." It might be far more real and far more impacting to simply be kind to one another. Or, as the Talmud says, "Deeds of kindness are equal in weight to all the commandments."

A loving heart

**Where there is the greatest love,
there are always miracles.**

WILLA CATHER

LOVE IS THE GREAT DEFINER OF LIFE. Those who love, live. Those who live and never learn to love are already dead of soul.

Learning to love is the challenge of a lifetime because it requires us to think about something other than ourselves, to make something other than ourselves the center of our lives. Clearly it is a learned art.

It's easy to find a crowd to run around with. It's one of the miracles of life, though, to find someone with whom we can share our souls. To love someone is to double all our joys, to divide all our disappointments. To be loved is to increase our courage and decrease our fears.

Real love grows. It is never at its inception what it is later as it becomes more spiritual, less physical, more one and less two, more supportive than supported.

Real love never sets out to possess the other. Real love frees the other to be the fullness of themselves. If you love someone, set them free.

The real love of two, if we hold it in healthy hands, makes us fearless, makes us even more loving, expands our hearts rather than contracts them and so enables us to take in the entire universe.

Love is all we know of God. It is all the proof we need of God. It is the sight of God in our own lives. Love something then; love anything and everything in order to release the best of yourself. No doubt about it: It is love that makes us human.

A mindful heart

**The miracle of life is not to walk on water.
The miracle is to walk on the green earth
in the present moment, to appreciate the
peace and beauty that are available now.**

THICH NHAT HANH

MINDFULNESS, the awareness of the sacredness
of the details of life, makes haste and trumpery impossible. It makes every act a sacred act.

Once we begin to be aware of the particles of life,
there is nothing most people call "major" that can
drain us of the best of it—the little things that make
up the elements of love and family and being.

Details are the small things that make the important things important: the extra cherry on the
birthday cake, the twist of the wrist in ballet, the
deep blue in the painting, the cocked head on

the family dog. "Love's first step," the philosopher Simone Weil wrote, "is attention."

Failing to notice one rose, we fail to notice the entire cosmos. We erode the earth under our feet and the air around us without even knowing that it is happening. We poison ourselves and have not a clue what culprit is doing it. We are all miracles living on a miracle called the earth. It is only a matter of coming to recognize what that means, both to us and to the rest of the people of the world.

Focusing on one thing in nature every day—one rose in a beautiful vase, one old tree gnarled but indomitable, one rugged mountain range undiminished by time, or whatever it is that calls us to reverence the mystery that is life—is meditation enough to make life precious whatever its stressors.

A mystical heart

**The Christian of the future will be
a mystic or will not exist at all.**

KARL RAHNER

MYSTICISM IS THE DEVELOPMENT of a sense
of cosmic consciousness, the awareness that we are
part of all that is. A cosmic worldview and a sense
of cosmic consciousness are not the same thing.
A cosmic worldview simply realizes that there is a
world bigger than the world of the self. Cosmic consciousness, on the other hand, is the realization that
as part of that world, I am created to be responsible
for the world.

The eyes of the mystic see God in every face,
find God in every place, seek God in every new
act of creation. They brim with love. The heart of
the mystic is the heart that breaks with every other
broken heart on earth.

The mystic does not separate any part of creation from the Creator. Non-human life is treated with the same kind of sacred reverence as is the human. Human life is treated with awe. Life becomes the filter through which God becomes present to the human eye. If we were a world of mystics, there would be no such thing as poverty in Africa, ecological disaster in the rain forests and oceans, racism in the West.

"In this," the mystic Julian of Norwich said of the acorn in her hand, "is everything there is and everything that will ever be." To recognize the oneness of life to this extent is soul-sightedness raised to a level of stunning awareness.

A non-judgmental heart

**Because you were bitten by a snake,
you fear a rope in the road.**

SUFI SAYING

WHEN WE SPEND OUR LIVES guarding ourselves against what might happen rather than
opening ourselves to what may happen, we poison
the well of the heart.

Suspicion says as much about us as it does about
the other. It marks us as people who are more inter-
ested in the sins of the other than in our own.

To judge another without either the experience
or evidence that confirms it is to draw boundaries
around our own lives. Better, perhaps, to be fooled
by someone than to be cut off by the cancer of un-
substantiated suspicion from the possibilities the
relationship might well bring.

Learning not to prejudge people and things is easy. All we need to do is to make a list of the judgments we've already made that were incorrect—all the right people who turned out to be wrong for us, the good things we insisted on having that turned out to be bad for us, the things we knew were absolutely correct that turned out to be absolutely incorrect. If that doesn't cure us of our tendency to stereotype and judge, nothing will.

To be happy it is necessary to learn to let go of the way we are convinced life is and open our hearts and mind to what really is. To live is to venture beyond our fears to taste the sweetness of the unknown.

An open heart

Who knows most, doubts most.

ROBERT BROWNING

CLOSED-MINDEDNESS is the capacity to be closed to every mind but my own. Which is a very small reservoir of knowledge, indeed.

It is not that information is not available. It is simply that we fail to seek it out, to listen to opposing viewpoints, to imagine another way. There is almost nothing on earth that can be done only one way—except, perhaps, the addition of 2 + 2 (and even that shifts!). But we love to act as if there were.

The need to be right too often supersedes the need to be open to the ideas of those around us. It is the disease of power and self-righteousness that is the terminal disease of human relationships.

When we refuse to say "you're wrong" or "I'm

right" to anything—when we learn to say instead: "I have always thought" and "Tell me why you say that"—we give ourselves the opportunity to learn something.

We grow up learning what we call the truths of our culture. When we begin to learn the truths of other cultures, we discover that truth is the sum total of everything, not the institutionalized doctrines of any one part of it.

Stretching ourselves beyond the boundaries of our family, our race, our nation, and our religion brings us to the point where we become citizens of the world. Just exactly what we were meant to be to begin with.

A passionate heart

**Only passions, great passions,
can elevate the soul to great things.**

DENIS DIDEROT

WE NEED A PASSION FOR LIFE, a surge of gratitude so deep that we will do whatever it takes to guarantee the fullness of life for the entire world.

Those with a passion for life have saved the world for us all. Helen Keller's passion saved the deaf. Florence Nightingale's passion saved the sick. Martin Luther King Jr.'s passion saved Black America. The question for us now is a simple one: What passion of ours is saving the world at the present time?

It is our passion for something beyond ourselves that keeps us alive. It gives a purpose to life that is far beyond breathing. It makes us into the human beings we were meant to be.

The test of what it is to be truly alive is the determination of what has meaning to us. What makes us cry? What makes us angry? What gives us sorrow? What gives us joy? "Live to the point of tears," Albert Camus wrote. Live, in other words, as if the life of the rest of the world depended on yours.

Let your passion be your guide to what it means to be great of soul in our time and place. Anything else is not living in the here and now. It is only the fact of being alive. Do not spend your life on small questions.

Passion is another word for love. If you haven't loved enough yet, by all means begin now. For your own sake.

A patient heart

**Only with a burning patience can we
conquer the splendid city which will give light,
justice and dignity to all.** ARTHUR RIMBAUD

PATIENCE TEACHES TWO LESSONS. One is
possibility; the other is acceptance. Either what's
possible will happen and our patience will be re-
warded, or we will learn to accept the fact that there
is something yet to be dealt with in the experience.

"To bear wrongs patiently" is not a sign of weakness. It is simply proof that self-knowledge and
self-criticism make us better people. Once we know
who we are—with all our weaknesses and all our own
mistakes—it becomes eminently clear that we can
afford to be patient with others. It is important to realize that those whose wrongs we bear are so often
bearing wrongs themselves, the weight of which

makes even more effort impossible. At least for now.

We do not "bear wrongs patiently" in order to ignore them or to be able to avoid dealing with them. We bear wrongs patiently in order to enable natural growth to succeed where forced growth so often fails in the long run.

To bear wrongs patiently does not mean that we do not work for justice. It simply means that we must work for justice justly. We must model what we want for others.

St. Teresa of Avila, a woman whose ideas were obstructed often in her own life, knew the power of holy patience. She wrote: "Let nothing disturb thee / Let nothing frighten thee / All things are changing / God alone is changeless / Patience attains the goal. / One who has God lacks nothing / God alone fills all our needs." The lesson is clear: If we proceed with patience, we will have everything we need spiritually, however much justice we must go on struggling for, as we go.

A peaceful heart

There can be no real peace without justice.
And without resistance there will be no justice.

ARUNDHATI ROY

PEACE, IN A WORLD BENT ON WAR and intent on drawing the rest of us into it, is a precious commodity. But not an easy one to achieve.

Do anything you can to avoid war—personal or public. Do everything you can to make peace real. But remember that peace can never come from either fear or threat. Both of those must be dispelled before the trust that is of the essence of peace can possibly break out.

Peace is not the acceptance of evil. On the contrary, real peace requires resistance to evil. But not in evil ways. This kind of peacemaking requires courage not power, a kind of strength that uses love rather than force to change the world.

It is possible for one person to refuse to make war, but it is not possible for one person to make peace. To make real peace takes two. To solve an impasse with the other, I need to ask myself what it is in me that is feeding the war.

At the basis of peace is respect for the traditions, cultures, gifts, and good intentions of the other. Anything else is either patronizing or arrogant. The greatest instrument of peace is language. When our words are kind—however difficult the message may be—peace is possible. When our words are hurtful, the peace between us will never be real.

To bring people to reconciliation, to avoid what is damaging to the other, to bring love where pain has been, to open our arms to the world—these make the Christian message real. It is time to stop defining peace as the absence of war and start defining it as the presence of God.

A prayerful heart

**Jesus went out to a
lonely place where he prayed.**

MARK 1:35

THERE ARE BOOKS APLENTY written on the subject of prayer, of course, but I have come to the point where I doubt that anybody can really "teach" anybody how to pray. That, I figure, is what life does. We can learn prayer forms, of course, but we do not learn either the function or the purpose of prayer until life drags us to it, naked and in pain.

Theologians of the late nineteenth and early twentieth century were very good at dissecting prayer. There was spoken prayer, silent prayer, prayer of the mind, prayer of the heart, and union with God, they told us. It all seems pretty amusing to me now. I was trying to learn to pray exactly the same way I learned to run a printing press. By the book. In both cases I discovered that the best way to learn to do it was to do it for a long, long time.

Most important of all though, at least for me, was the line in the *Rule of Benedict* that instructs the monastic community to keep prayer brief and the monastics to leave chapel quietly so that anybody who wants to stay behind for private prayer can do so without interruption. In those two simple statements I learned enough about prayer to last me for a lifetime: First, that in order to learn to pray we need to do it regularly. And second, that real contemplative prayer starts where formal prayer ends.

Point: Prayer is not a "technique." It is an attitude of mind, a quality of soul, and a dimension of the daily.

A purposeful heart

True happiness is not attained through self-gratification but through fidelity to a worthy purpose. HELEN KELLER

THERE IS A DIFFERENCE between having a purpose in life and having a job in life.

Everyone has been given something of skill or personality, of mind or artistry, of insight or wisdom that is meant to be spent on the rest of the world. It's not meant to be our job; it's meant to be our life. If what we love to do and do well happens to be our job, lucky us. If, on the other hand, our job simply supports our ability to follow our passion, lucky us. If we have a job but have not bothered to develop our passion, not only are we unlucky but so is the world that depends on us to do what we were born to do. Finding where we fit, what we're meant to do, what it is our heart seeks is both the task and the measure of a happy life.

Life without a purpose greater than myself is an empty shell. The purpose of life is to do something with others, for others, and because of others that makes the world a better place to be because each of us has been there.

If you want to know how to find real purpose in life, ask yourself what needs to be done and do it. What is it you hope for in this century? A sustainable planet? A world where every child has enough food and decent shelter? A world where women are free to make their own adult decisions? The preservation of oceans? A world without war? The end of pollution? Good—now what are you doing to help achieve that?

To find purpose in life that engages us heart and soul and body, we must begin. Willa Cather wrote, "This is happiness: To be dissolved into something completely great."

A questioning heart

In a room where people unanimously maintain a conspiracy of silence, one word of truth sounds like a pistol shot.

CZESLAW MILOSZ

THE QUALITY OF LIFE AS WE KNOW IT has changed radically in our lifetime. When I was a young woman, the world—my world—was an exercise in answers. We had absolute answers for everything: who was going to heaven and who was not. The number of planets and how they went together. The age of the earth and how it developed. But now things have changed. Now, it seems, life is more an exercise in questions than a catalogue of certainties. It is the unending process of an expanding universe and its expanding knowledge with it. Nothing, it seems, is not now open to question.

When we consider yesterday's answers more important than today's questions, we fail both the past and the future. In the first place, the past was for its own time; in the second place, it is meant to prepare us to face the future.

Never refuse to ask a question however unwelcome the question may be. In the end, it may be the only thing that saves us from our own ignorance. To keep growing, it is imperative to keep asking the forbidden questions.

When we try to stop thought by stopping people from asking forbidden questions, we only prove the paucity of our answers. What is true will hold up to scrutiny—however much untruth is around us. If an idea be of God—like love and goodness and openness and respect and tolerance and compassion—it will thrive in the most godless environment.

A reflective heart

Know thyself.

SOCRATES

EVERYBODY GROWS UP LEARNING about themselves from others. As in "This is Tom, our oldest. He's the lazy one." Or "This is Lisa, our youngest. Nothing but a scamp." Or "This is Mike. He's the smartest of our kids." These are the things we remember all our lives. For better or for worse.

Most of what we heard about ourselves from those around us as we grew up is probably at least a bit true. But the important thing to realize, as we grow, is that none of it is all true.

There is a great deal more to us than most of us know—or give ourselves the opportunity to find out. Coming to know the self is the grand excursion of growing up. We have to know what we believe and want and desire before we can even begin to be a person. But that comes as much through experience as it does through books.

Self-knowledge is what teaches us how much we yet have to learn. It is one of life's more difficult lessons, without which we succumb to arrogance and die from pretentiousness. Not to mention loneliness.

Coming to know ourselves and bringing what we are to fullness of soul is the task of a lifetime. "Our true life," Tagore wrote, "lies at a great depth within us." We are, in other words, much more than we think we are, and we are meant to become it.

A scarred heart

Birds make great circles of their freedom.
How do they learn it?
They fall, and falling, they're given wings.

RUMI

IF WE ALLOW OURSELVES TO LEARN from it, failure is its own kind of success.

God doesn't have to punish pride; pride will make it impossible for us to learn from anybody else. And lust will make love impossible. And greed will make contentment impossible. And covetousness will make serenity impossible. And anger will make inner peace impossible. But all of them will give us a depth of understanding we might never have achieved otherwise. It is what we learn from our failures that brings us to new levels of holiness.

To fall is to have the opportunity to begin again, wiser this time. Failure is not the end of life. It is the beginning of another way of living. The function of failure is to stretch us beyond what is expected to what is possible.

Failure is the lesson that teaches me that I am not self-sufficient. It gives me the opportunity to recognize the gifts of others and depend on them.

Beware of an addiction to perfection—it either fools us or breaks us. It can fool us into thinking that we really are "perfect," or it can precipitate a breakdown when we finally have to admit that we're not.

When we finally begin to be comfortable with failure, we are free to try everything in life. We become explorers of the multiple paths to happiness we may not have found if we had not failed in so many areas.

There is really no such thing as failure. There is only the opportunity to find more of ourselves, more of the journey to God, in life. Both of which take courage.

A seeking heart

Seek God, not where God lives.

DESERT SAYINGS

THE SEARCH FOR GOD comes one day to the point where we know without a doubt that we are immersed in God. Bringing ourselves to finally recognize that is the essential task of life.

There is no such thing as "getting" God. The fact is that we already have God. God is not somewhere else. God is everywhere. God is here. With me. In me. Now. It is the awareness of that presence which life intends to teach us to cultivate.

There's nothing wrong with feeling that God is absent. Then, at least, we know that our soul is alive and going in the right direction. The God of Light is also the God of Darkness. Why would we not expect God, then, to be in the dark spots of our lives as well as in its light?

To be centered in God alone does not mean to have no interests but God. It means to realize that all other interests are meant to bring us closer to God. They are not meant to take God's place in our lives but to enable God's spirit to enhance the meaning of everything else.

The point at which we look beyond ourselves is where we find God in the rest of the world. Then life spills over with the wonder of God. Then we find the fullness of the Spirit for which we have been searching.

Once we begin to recognize God at work in us, everything in life becomes holy, becomes life-giving. Then God is not an occasional find in life—in church, maybe, or at a sunset. God is a sense of life now and of life beyond life. God is what calls me to live into the heart of the universe.

A self-realized heart

Learn what you are and be such.

PINDAR

THE SELF IS FORMED one experience at a time. Choosing those wisely is of the essence of life. But experience without reflection is useless. The constant question of life must be: What did I learn from this? It takes a great deal of courage to scrutinize the driving forces of the self and then muster up the internal freedom it takes to redirect them.

Coming to know ourselves is the beginning of both humility and freedom. After that, we have no one to impress but ourselves. It is the lesson of a lifetime. When we learn to be more tomorrow than we have been today, we are on our way to being free to go on becoming more of ourselves always.

When we are free enough to refuse to remain

what we have always been, we are ready to love someone else. The freedom to be the self is what makes it possible to love anyone else and deserve their love in return.

Until we have become the best of ourselves, we are not really capable of becoming good for anyone else. Good relationships free us to become the best of ourselves; they do not enslave us to the demands or the dependencies of others.

Whatever we are, it will continue to bubble up within us—however much anyone tries to suppress it, however much we ourselves try to ignore it. It can take a lifetime of side roads to find the highways of the heart that take us home, whole and entire, satisfied and content.

A silent heart

Teach us to care and not to care.
Teach us to sit still. T.S. ELIOT

SILENCE IS WHERE WE MUST GO when we want to be truly spiritual people. Only there does God speak to the heart. But learning how to keep silent and when to keep silent—and when not to—is a great spiritual art.

Hard and bitter silence refuses to allow another person the chance to change the position that has hurt me. It refuses, as well, to allow me to understand the needs of those around me. Soft and pliant silence makes it possible for the other to speak. More than that, it enables me to see the world from someone else's point of view.

Calm and receptive silence invites the ideas of those around me. It gives them dignity and value. It gives me another side to my personality.

Silence that is cowardly appears to agree with everyone but in the end contributes more to division than to unity. It questions nothing, understands nothing, advances nothing in a group. It is more about safety than it is about growth. "Sometimes," the graffiti artist wrote, "silence is not golden—just yellow."

Silence requires us to attend to the turmoil within us. It refuses to allow us to ignore our own greatest questions in life. The silence that seeks to bury our secrets from ourselves only eats away at our own souls.

There is no virtue in keeping silence in the face of injustice. That kind of silence only makes us either the accomplice or the thrall of those who refuse to allow another truth to be spoken. The silence we keep in the company of evil is evil. Truth spoken out of the hot center of the cave of silence is always a gift.

A simple heart

Those who have cattle have care.

KENYAN PROVERB

THE FACT IS THAT we do come into the world empty-handed and we go out the same way, so why do we spend so much of life trying to acquire things? The need to have things and control others is insidious. It is a worm in the heart that dooms us to restlessness and discontent. It means that nothing is ever good enough for us. We have missed the fine art of "letting go" and the freedom that comes with it.

Desiring little, there is nothing that can really be taken from us. When we spend our lives attempting to acquire what we do not need and even seldom use, we waste our strength on things that neither stretch our souls nor satisfy our hearts. Look around you. Do you have everything you need? Then why are you exhausting yourself trying to get more? Learn to enjoy what you have and you will have everything life has to give.

Simplicity is not the fine art of reducing the world to the groundless elementary. It is the high art of considering all of life and taking from it only what constitutes real beauty, genuine support, and true assessment of everything in life.

Simplicity is honesty, about life, about ourselves. Being who we are rather than becoming who everybody else says we must be is the ultimate simplicity. Nothing is more difficult to acquire in life.

The simple person puts on no airs, requires no special attention, dominates no conversations, lives quietly and responsibly, seldom seeks the services of others, and, even more so, seldom requires the best of anything, let alone everything.

A stable heart

**To be rooted is perhaps the most important and
least recognized need of the human soul.**

SIMONE WEIL

STABILITY IS THE COMPASS OF THE HEART.
It keeps our souls pointing to whatever it is that
gives us direction and fulfillment. To give ourselves
to a never-changing, totally defining goal is not easy,
but it is essential if we ever want to really live, rather
than simply wanting to go on breathing.

It is the defining of the dream out of the dust of
long-standing dailiness that is the real definition of
stability. It is not a physical thing entirely. It is the
determination to follow the primal dream wherever
it leads, whatever it costs.

Stability is not a false choice between staying here
or going there. It is the hard choice I must eventu-

ally make between being what I am and doing what I am supposed to do. One of the functions of stability is to steep us in the responsibilities of the present, to garner from us a commitment to the future. Stability is not another word for "recluse." It is a synonym for involvement in the here and now.

Only those whose hearts are stable, whose souls have a clear end in view, can possibly be trusted to risk changing their work, their goals, their minds, and what they call home.

Stability is the home of the heart. It is what enables us to move on to where the heart is going. Ultimately, stability frees us because it roots us so deeply in something, somewhere, that no matter what happens as we go through life, there is nothing that can deter us.

To be firmly formed in something, it is necessary to be deeply grounded in it—a relationship, a system, a discipline, a work—for years. Stability is the apprenticeship of life.

A trusting heart

**Teacher, does it not concern you
that we are going to drown?**

MARK 4:38

WHEN THE STORMS OF LIFE ASSAIL US, our
first temptation is to quit life, to be delivered from
"this vale of tears." We have no time for darkness,
no love for doubt. We want to live unlimited by
anything. But limitation may be the very thing that
leads us to create our new and better selves.

When we realize that storms are part of life, not
interruptions of life, we can live from one to the
other with real equanimity, growing stronger all
the time. How much better to die whole than only
half-developed?

The storms of life are what lead us to look for
help. That's not weakness; that's simply the admis-

sion that being human requires us to be connected to the rest of the human race. Never fail to ask for help when you need it. Those who swallow a stone become a stone. When we insist on denying our needs, we deny our own humanity to such a point that one day we wake up and we're not really human anymore. We are simply lumps of stone where warmth and joy and growth should be.

Sometimes we only look for God when we are in the midst of one of life's great storms. In that case, blessed be life's great storms.

Once we have survived one of the great storms of life, we come to realize that we can survive all of them—not because God intervened to save us but because God gave us the strength to save ourselves.

God always cares for us, but God does not always care for us the way we want to be cared for at the time. And, in the end, we may discover that was the greatest caring of them all.

A truthful heart

The truth will set you free.

JOHN 8:32

WHEN WE HIDE THE TRUTH that is inside of us, we hide the part of us that stands the best chance of really contributing something valuable to the rest of the world. To die fully alive, it is surely necessary to claim our own truth in the face of other truths, to stand alone when only standing alone can possibly define the whole breadth of thought on a subject, to be able to speak into the face of one concern the wisdom of another.

Independence of mind is bought at high cost: It requires us to be able to trust our own motives for speaking. It also requires the ability to learn from the thinking of others. Otherwise, we doom ourselves to be either the clone of another or simply a teenage replica of ourselves.

It is fear of the other, not our doubt of the truth, that is most inclined to gag our souls. But it has its limits. "Before I was twenty," the wag wrote, "I worried about what my teachers would think of me. When I was twenty, I worried about what my parents would think of me. When I was thirty, I worried about what my boss would think of me. When I was forty, I worried about what the neighbors would think of me. But when I got to be fifty, I discovered that nobody was standing around thinking about me at all."

Don't be afraid to speak. Be afraid what will happen to the whole truth if you don't.

An unchained heart

Only one thing made him happy and now that it was gone everything made him happy.

LEONARD COHEN

LIFE IS MADE UP OF MANY PARTS. When we allow one part of it to become the whole of it, the other parts of our souls atrophy. We walk around half-dead and never even know it.

The parts of life which we have not developed are the very things that are calling us most clearly to become more than we are. It's when we immerse ourselves in the rest of life that we grow the most. To be obsessed by anything means to stunt our own growth to the point of a tiny moment in time. It leaves us breathing but not alive.

Narrow-mindedness, for instance, is a type of obsession. When we refuse to think that anything might be done differently, we have locked ourselves into a single period of life while our minds go to mold.

When the heart is open, the mind is free to become the most of what it is. When we lose what we think we cannot possibly do without, we are finally free.

We're all on the verge of obsession with something that entrances us and captivates us and, eventually, fails us. One of the core questions of life is: What is it in us that so captures our souls, our thoughts, our feelings, that it makes consciousness of the rest of life impossible?

That is the question on which tomorrow depends. The hard part is that each of us must answer it for ourselves.

An understanding heart

**We want people to feel with us
more than to act for us.**

GEORGE ELIOT

THE LOWEST LEVEL OF HUMANITY is to demand reasons for a person's behavior. The next level of humanity is to accept excuses. The highest level of humanity is to understand the soulfulness of a person's motives however disjointed they may be, and love them despite their motive.

But we develop understanding slowly. It is, it seems, a by-product of experience, a gesture of otherness, an acceptance of fallibility.

It's when we come to understand ourselves—our own fears, our own demons, our own struggles—that we have the best chance of understanding others. When we have suffered enough to understand the sufferings of others, we are closer to peace, nearer to justice, more ready to love than we have ever been before.

Once we understand that we are all pretending to be what we cannot ever be—perfectly unique and uniquely perfect—then we can finally give way to the gradual growth that life is all about. It's only when we refuse to accept the whole of the human condition that we reject others and despise ourselves as well.

As C.S. Lewis says, "Friendship is born at that moment when one person says to another, 'What! You too? I thought I was the only one!'" We are all capable of everything because we are all made of the same inherently imperfect stuff—humanity.

To be understanding is to open ourselves to the woundedness—and therefore, the incipient holiness—of the world.

A wise heart

**The years teach much
which the days never knew.**

RALPH WALDO EMERSON

IN THE BOOK OF PROVERBS, we are instructed to "get wisdom." Wisdom, in other words, is not a free gift. We are told to develop it. We are, then, required to seek meaning in life, to understand that life is not a series of events. Life is a series of learnings. Wisdom is what we are meant to cull from every event in life.

Wisdom is the depth of soul that enables us to understand what must remain in our lives when everything else—the job, the health, the security, the excitement—goes, as all those things someday, inevitably, will. Lin Tang says, "The wisdom of life consists in the elimination of the nonessentials."

It is what we believe spiritually that carries us through life. It is the well of wisdom from which we are meant to draw. We must be careful as we seek wisdom not to confuse the spiritual with the religious. Religious rigidity and self-righteousness have destroyed a great deal in life. Only that which nurtures the truly spiritual in us, the search for the presence of God in every small dimension of life, is real wisdom.

If, by the time we die, beauty has moved the silent center of us, love has wracked our hearts, and the word of God has seeped into our heart, we will be as wise as any human being can ever hope to be.

Also by Joan Chittister

Songs of the Heart • *Reflections on the Psalms*

Sister Joan offers poignant, challenging reflections on 25 psalms, each offering a spiritual oasis away from the stresses of the world. In praying and reflecting on these psalms, readers will find new meaning at the core of life. Great spiritual reading for all who long to pray the psalms more deeply and attentively.

HARDCOVER | 136 PAGES | $12.95 | 978-1-58595-835-1

God's Tender Mercy • *Reflections on Forgiveness*

Here Sister Joan tackles the virtue of mercy and its vital connection to forgiveness. She invites readers to stop judging, accusing, and criticizing "sinners," and to see themselves in their number. This challenging and inspiring book is spiritual reading at its very best.

HARDCOVER | 80 PAGES | $10.95 | 978-1-58595-799-6

The Breath of the Soul • *Reflections on Prayer*

This simple yet profound book is an examination of what we ourselves must bring to the discipline of prayer—whatever form it takes—in order to make prayer a deep and integral part of our lives. Great spiritual reading for all who long for prayer to be at the core of their lives.

HARDCOVER | 144 PAGES | $12.95 | 978-1-58595-747-7

1-800-321-0411
www.23rdpublications.com

TWENTY
THIRD 23rd
PUBLICATIONS